I Read You Loud and Clear

THE KIDS' WORLD ALMANAC®
OF COLORFUL PHRASES

I Read You Loud and Clear

THE KIDS' WORLD ALMANAC® OF COLORFUL PHRASES

ELYSE SOMMER

Illustrations by
JOHN
KERSCHBAUM

WORLD ALMANAC

AN IMPRINT OF PHAROS BOOKS • A SCRIPPS HOWARD COMPANY

NEW YORK

Copyright © 1990 by Elyse Sommer
Illustrations copyright © 1990 by Pharos Books

First published in 1990.

Library of Congress Cataloging-in-Publication Data

Sommer, Elyse.
    I read you loud and clear: the Kids' World Almanac® of colorful
phrases
    by Elyse Sommer: illustrated by John Kerschbaum.
       p. cm.
    Summary: A thesaurus of phrases designed to provide
an appreciation for and understanding of idioms, similes, and
other colorful phrases.
    ISBN 0-88687-575-7 : $10.95
    1. English language--Terms and phrases--Juvenile literature.
[1. English language--Terms and phrases.] I. Kerschbaum, John,
ill. II. Title.
PE1689.S68 1990
423'.1--dc20   89-78437
                                           CIP
                                           AC

Printed in the United States of America

World Almanac
An Imprint of Pharos Books
A Scripps Howard Company
200 Park Avenue
New York, NY 10166

10 9 8 7 6 5 4 3 2 1

Cover and interior design by Bea Jackson.
Cover and interior illustrations by John Kerschbaum.

Contents

A Thank You and An Invitation

Our special thanks to our junior editorial team: Stacey Robin Beck, Michael David Kass, Lauren M. Lang, Barry O'Donnell, Robyn M. Reiter, and the students in Heather Margolis's and Helen Kempler's second and fourth grades. These junior editors who range in age from 7 to 11 performed many important jobs. Here are some of the things they did:

- Read and rated more than twenty-five pages of phrases,
- Tested the phrases out on their friends and classmates,
- Scouted their neighborhoods for phrases that were not included but which should have been,
- Added new twists to existing phrases and invented many brand-new ones.

You too can become a junior editor for the next edition of The Kids' World Almanac of Colorful Phrases. Just make a copy of this form and fill in as many lines as possible (yes, yes, yes, you can use any old sheet of paper if you need more space!). Under **Source** put one of the following:

Me if you made it up...**N/S** if you heard it around your neighborhood or school...**B** if you saw it in a book...**X** for any other source.

The best original phrases sent in will be included in the next edition. Send your contributions to:

Elyse Sommer
P.O. Box 1133
Forest Hills, NY 11375

Phrases to Include   Sources

1. _____

2. _____

3. _____

4. _____

5. _____

6. _____

7. _____

8. _____

9. _____

10. _____

Introduction
What It's All About

When someone uses a colorful expression it lands on the ear or the page with a satisfying and resounding smack. At its best it contains crisp, zippy words that draw an imaginary picture. It has the snap, crackle, and pop that adds flavor to what you say and write, as spices add flavor to what you eat.

This thesaurus combines the three most common types of colorful expressions:

Idioms. These don't always mean exactly what the words used say but are used so frequently that they're understood anyway. The idiom owes its popularity to a combination of sight and sound appeal. The sight appeal comes from the picture the words bring to mind. The sound appeal comes from the way the words sound together. Sound appeal is sometimes helped along by alliteration, which means that one or more words begin with the same sound. For example: **raise the roof,** a phrase in which both key words begin with an "r" sound.

Many idioms start out meaning something very specific to a special group of people but end up being used by everyone. At that point no one pays much attention to the idiom's original meaning. Two phrases which illustrate this process are **on one's toes** or **face the music**. Both were once used only by people in the theatre but are now used by anyone who's alert or courageous enough to accept a difficult situation.

Similes. The simile makes an idea more colorful by comparing two unlike things. An example would be to compare the resemblance between two friends to the peas in a pea pod (**alike as two peas in a pod**). The comparison is usually introduced with the word *as* or *like*. Like idioms, similes frequently last longer than their original meanings and rely on alliteration for extra sound appeal. **Sure as shooting** is a good example of an alliterative simile that no longer means what it once did.

Slang. Both idioms and similes are short cuts for expressing popular or common thoughts. This is doubly true for slang expressions that reduce a longer phrase to a shorter phrase, or to just one word. Even more than idioms and similes, slang tends to originate with a special group of people, usually as a sort of secret language. Many a slang expression lasts only long enough for a new one to come along to take its place. Many are used in only one part of the United States. The really popular ones eventually become accepted as part of our everyday informal speech. At that point they are added to general or special slang dictionaries.

How To Make the Most of This Book

Whether you use an idiom, a simile, or a slang expression to make a point, always remember that even the most colorful phrase loses some of its punch if it's used too much. Such once terrific and now too-familiar expressions are known as clichés (*klee shays*). That doesn't mean that cliches don't have their good points. Because everybody knows what they mean, they provide a fast and easy way to make yourself understood. More important, with a little thought and imagination you can give new life to a worn-out phrase. And so, if you've already heard or used some of the phrases included here, why not try to give them that new twist of your own. Once you do, you've taken the first step towards becoming an original phrase maker.

How To Use This Book

A thesaurus doesn't give a precise definition of each entry as a dictionary does. Instead it groups words together according to their meanings. To help you get the most use and enjoyment from this collection of colorful phrases, each group of phrases in the phrase section is arranged alphabetically by headings. These main headings, printed in **heavy type** will give you the general meaning of the phrases that follow. Some groups of phrases include additional headings which describe the phrases underneath more exactly. These subheadings are indented and set in bold face.

Sometimes you will want to compare one group of phrases with another related group. The words *See Also:* will point you in the right direction. For example, **To Be Angry** includes a *See also:*, to lead you to **To Annoy** and **To Be Disgusted**.

Because there's often more than one possible heading under which you might search for a phrase, the thesaurus includes many extra headings. These extra main headings are also printed in heavy type and are listed in alphabetical order. They do not have phrase entries but they are followed by the word *See:* and one or more **main headings** that do contain phrase entries. To show you how it works, suppose you're looking for a clever answer to someone who brags to you or insults you. Try the heading **To Answer Back**. You won't find any phrases, but you will find

> *See:* **Insults**
> **To Stop**
> **Talking**
> **Zappers**

To check if and where a phrase you know is listed, turn to the Index at the end of the book. This lists every phrase in alphabetical order.

To sum up, in The Phrases section, everything is alphabetized according to headings; these headings describe the general meaning of the phrases that follow. In the Index the individual phrases are alphabetized. Both the headings in The Phrases section and the phrases in the Index are alphabetized by the *main word* or *idea*.

And Don't Forget To Remember. . .

- You can browse through the book from front to back, back to front, or start and stop any place.
- The headings in the main section are alphabetized but the phrases themselves are not. Instead, the phrases are organized so that those with the same key words are together.
- Whether you read the main section from A through Z, and stop wherever a phrase strikes your fancy, or whether you look up phrases to fit a specific idea, be sure to read the section between the phrases and the Index: From Phrase Seeker to Phrase Maker.

- Both the main headings and the phrases in the Index are alphabetized by the main word or idea. It's as if words like *to* and *to be* were not included at all.

I Read You Loud and Clear

THE KIDS' WORLD ALMANAC®
OF COLORFUL PHRASES

The
Phrases

Note: Additional information for phrases marked with the symbol ☐ can be found in the boxed-off text nearby

To Abandon *See:* To Desert

To Admit *See:* To Confess

To Agree *see* eye to eye ☐1, on the same wave length ☐1.
Agree after you disagree: bury the hatchet.
    See also: To Go Together

To Be Alert *See:* To Be Attentive, To Be Smart

To Be Alike alike as two drops of water, alike as two peas in a pod ☐2, alike as the pills in a medicine bottle, be the spitting image of someone.

> When you see **eye to eye** with someone, you both see or think about something in the same way. In the language of television, where each channel has different wave lengths, you're tuned to the same channel or **the same wave length**.

> **Alike as two peas in a pod**, like many of our favorite phrases, has both sight and sound appeal. The two "p" words add a nice snappy sound to the picture of the look-alike peas.

To Be Angry   burned up, ticked off, get one's back up, in a huff, on the ceiling.

> **To be very angry:**   blow one's top, blow one's stack ③, blow a fuse ③, blow up, fit to be tied, hit the ceiling, hot under the collar ③, mad as a wet hen, wild as a fire, raise the roof, see red, sore as a boil.

> **To make angry:**   get under one's skin, to be a pain in the neck, to be a royal pain.

> > *See also:* To Annoy, To Be Disgusted

To Annoy   push a button, drive up the wall.

> **To be annoying:**   annoying as hiccups, annoying as a persistent itch.

> > *See also:* To Be Angry, To Be Disgusted, To Tease

To Answer Back   *See:* To Stop, Talking, Zapping or Giving Smart Answers

To Be Anxious   *See:* To Be Scared, To Worry

Appearance   *See:* To Be Alike, To Be Dressed Up, To Be Nice Looking, To Be Sloppy Looking

To Argue   *See:* To Disagree

To Attempt   *See:* To Try

To Be Attentive   keep one's eye on the ball, watchful as a dog waiting for a bone, attentive as a musician in an orchestra, on one's toes.

---

3   **Hot under the collar** describes a physical sign of anger. To **blow ones stack** or to **blow a fuse** compare anger to a smokestack spitting out smoke and an over-worked electrical system.

Watchful as a dog waiting for a bone

To tell someone to pay attention: read my lips, wake up!

To tell someone that you're listening: (often used by someone who doesn't really mean it): I hear you, I read you, I'm all ears, I dig you.

   See also: To Be Smart

To Avoid Doing or Saying Something   beat around the bush, to be slippery as an eel, to be slippery as a wet fish, to be slippery as slush, spin one's wheels.

Awful   awful as losing your best friend, the pits, positively grossitating.

To Be Beautiful *See:* To Be Nice Looking

To Belong *See:* To Go Together, To Fit

To Be Bent/Crooked bent like a rainbow, bent like the letter "S", crooked as a snake.

To Bewilder *See:* To Be Confusing

To Be Big big as a planet, big as a braggart's mouth, big as a brontosaurus, large as life.

    See also: To Be Tall

Black black as coal, black as night, black as a poodle's nose, black as a blackbird.

To Blow Up *See:* To Exaggerate

Blue blue as the sky, blue as blueberry pie.

To Be Boring as boring as watching paint dry, as boring as boiled potatoes, a yawn and a half, a big yawn, a fast forward 4.

Anything that's **a fast forward** is so uninteresting that you'd like to push a button to skip it, the way you fast-forward the commercials of taped television shows.

4

To say that you're bored: my eyes glaze over (or abbreviate it to MEGO, pronounced *meh go)*, bored stiff.

A boring person: a white-bread (or white bready) personality.

To Bother   *See:* To Annoy

To Brag   toot one's own horn.

Bragging words: eat your heart out.

To Be Brave *See:* To Be Courageous

To Be Busy busy as a bee, busy as a beaver, busy as a frisbee at the beach, busy as a bouncing ball, busy as ants at a picnic, busy as a toy store before Christmas.

 See also: To Work Hard

Busy as a beaver

To Be Calm   calm as statue, not bat an eyelash, cooled out, cool as a breeze, keep one's cool, hang loose.
   To tell someone to act more calmly: cool it, chill out, take a chill pill, get a grip, take it easy, take it light.

To Be Cautious   cautious as a cat walking on egg shells, cautious as a thief in a store full of policemen, cover all bases, hedge one's bets, play it safe.

To Be Certain   in the bag, it's a cinch, sure as shooting [5], sure as one plus one makes two, sure as tricks at a magic show, sure as a burn will cause a blister, sure as shouting in a schoolyard, for sure [5], have something wired [5], you'd better believe it.

Sure as shooting and **it's a cinch** continue to be popular, even though they're no longer tied to their original meanings: to shoot straight and the cinch or strap used to keep a horse's saddle in place. **For sure** and **to have something wired** are newer ways to say the same thing.

5

To Change (one's attitude or behavior)   change one's tune[6], turn over a new leaf[6], eat one's words, shape up.

To Chase After   *See:* To Follow

To Be Clean   clean as a whistle [7], clean as a Band-Aid®, squeaky clean.

To Be Clear   clear as a bell, crystal clear, clear as sunshine, as plain as the nose on your face.
   See also: To Be Familiar, To Understand

Cling   *See:* Stick To

To Be Close   *See:* To Be Friendly

To Be Clumsy   all thumbs, have two left feet, clumsy as an elephant on roller skates, Captain Klutz.

To Be Cold   cold as ice, cold as outer space, cold as a frozen fish, cold as the North Pole, cold as the inside of a refrigerator.
   See also: To Be Unfriendly

Colors   *See:* Black, Blue, Green, Pink, Red, White, Yellow

To Come After   *See:* To Follow

Medieval minstrels often changed their tunes to fit their audience. Today to **change one's tune** refers to a change in attitude. A complete change is like beginning on a new, blank page or **turning over a new leaf**.

7

To be **clean as a whistle** is to be as spotlessly clean as a whistle must be to produce a clear sound. This expression has been part of our language since the 1700s. Look around you for other objects that would bring to mind a picture of cleanliness.

Clumsy as an elephant on roller skates

Comebacks   *See:* To Stop, Talking, Zapping or Giving Smart Answers

To Be Comfortable   snug as a bug in a rug, cozy as a quilt, comfortable as an old shoe, comfortable as being with your best friend, comfortable as a goodnight hug, cozy as a pillow on a bed.

To Be Commonplace   *See:* To Be Familiar

To Be Compatible   *See:* To Agree, To Go Together

To Complain   dump on.

Get together to complain: have a gripe session.

Completely   the whole ball of wax, all the way, but good, the whole nine yards.

To Compliment   *See:* To Flatter

To Be Conceited   *See:* To Be Vain

To Confess   get something off one's chest.

To confess reluctantly: cough up the truth.

See also: To Be Courageous

To Be Confusing   clear as mud, puzzling as a puzzle without clues.

To be confused: at sea, not know which end is up.

To Be Contented   *See:* To Be Happy

To Continue   *See:* To Go On

To Be Correct   *See:* To Be Right

To Be Courageous   fearless as a fireman, keep a stiff upper lip, screw up one's courage.

To accept a difficult situation or punishment: face the music⑧, face up to ⑧.

See also: To Try

To Be Cowardly   *See:* To Be Scared

To Be Crazy   crazy as a loon ⑨, looney tunes, nutty as a fruitcake, a number-one nutcase, off the wall, the elevator's not going to the top floor, the lights are on but no one's home, not wrapped too tight.

To be crazy or wild in one's behavior or enthusiasm: go bananas, flip out, freak out, whacked out, go ape.

8   When you don't run away from trouble, you **face the music** or you **face up to it**. The expression may have originated with a singer too nervous to face the musicians in the orchestra pit.

Go ape

Because the loon, a North American diving bird, has a wild cry, **crazy as a loon** is used to describe wild behavior. A modern variation is to say someone's a **looney tunes**.

9

To Criticize   *See:* To Scold

To Be Crooked   *See:* To Be Bent

To Be Crowded/Close Together   close as fingers inside a pair of mittens, close as Siamese twins, close as flies in a bottle, close as sardines, like a zoo.

To Be Cruel   *See:* To Be Mean, To Be Unfair

To Be Current   in sync, on top of, with it, that's cool, that's fresh, in the picture.

   See also: To Be Fresh, To Be Smart

To Daydream   *See:* To Be Inattentive

To Desert   leave high and dry .

> *See also:* To Discard

To Be Determined   hang in, hang tough, stubborn as a mule , stubborn as a stain.

> *See also:* To Try

To Be Difficult   difficult as trying to paint the wind, difficult as running with your feet tied, a tough nut to crack.

> *See also:* To Be Silly, To Be Useless

To Disagree   disagree (or fight) like cats and dogs, split like a torn pair of jeans, as far apart as the planets.

To have something to argue about: have a bone to pick, have some grass to mow, create a storm.

10

When someone leaves you **high and dry**, you're left on your own like a ship tossed by a storm onto dry land.

To Disappear gone with the wind, vanish into thin air, vanish like writing in the sand, disappear like raindrops in a drain, disappear like spit in the wind, disappear like a rainbow, go up in smoke.

See also: To Fail

To Discard drop (someone or something) like a used tissue, discard like a bad habit, hand someone a walking ticket, give someone the heave-ho.

To be discarded or excluded: Out of the loop.

To Discourage take the wind out of someone's sails, throw cold water on, put the whammy on.

To discourage with an evil stare: give someone the evil eye, give someone the fish eye.

To Be in Disgrace in the doghouse, in the boob loop.

See also: To Be in Trouble

To Be Disgusted fed up, have had it up to one's eyebrows (or eyeballs), have had it up to here, grossed out [11], scuzzed out [11], turned off.

Disgusted look: a you-must-be-out-of-your-mind face.

Disgusting person: slime bucket, sleaze ball.

To Be Dishonest lie like a tombstone, lie like a rug, lie like a thief.

A lie told out of politeness or kindness: a white lie.

To call someone a liar: liar, liar, your pants are on fire.

When you play around with words you often create a new catchphrase. For example, "that's a gross thing to do," was turned into **grossed out**. **Scuzzed out** is a variation of the "ess" sound.

A tough nut to crack

See also: To Exaggerate, Zapping or Giving Smart
Answers

To Be Dressed Up   all dolled up, all gussied up, all
spruced up, all duded up, putting on the dog, dressed up
like a sore finger, dressy as a Thanksgiving turkey.

See also: To Be Nice Looking

To Be Dumb   *See:* To Be Quiet, To Be Stupid

To Be Easy   easy as rolling off a log, easy as falling out of bed, easy as it is for a cat to have twins, easy as pointing a finger, easy as making a wish, easy as pie, a piece of cake, no sweat, no problem, a lead pipe cinch [12].

  See Also: To Be Certain

Eating   eat like a pig, eat like an elephant [13], eat your head off, eat yourself silly, eat like the fat man in a circus, pig out, a calorie cruncher.

12   **A lead pipe cinch** takes its meaning from the fact that plumbers use lead a lot because it's easy to work with. Like **it's a cinch** (*see* To Be Certain), it can also mean that something is a sure thing.

Full-grown elephants eat about 400 pounds of food per day. At the Bronx Zoo in New York that 400 pounds consists of 300 pounds of hay plus a hundred pounds of grains, stale bread, fruits and vegetables.   **13**

To eat very little: eat like a bird.

    See also: To Be Hungry

Effort   *See:* To Try

To Encourage   give someone the green light, give someone the go-ahead.

    Encourage someone to not do something: just say no.

    See also: To Praise Something or Someone, To Try

To Be Endless   *See:* To Go On

To Be Enthusiastic   all fired up, raring to go 14, hot to trot.

> **14** The word *raring* isn't in the dictionary even though **raring to go** is commonly used to describe someone eager to do something. The term was probably invented by someone who associated *raring* with horses rearing up and engines roaring.

Eat like a pig

To Exaggerate   make a mountain out of a molehill, stretch the truth, give someone a snow job [15], lay (or spread) it on thick, full of hot air [15], make a big production.

> **Someone who exaggerates:**   a big mouth, a truth stretcher.
>
> *See also:* To Be Dishonest

To Be Excited   go hog wild, get carried away, hyped up, lose one's cool.

> *See also:* To Be Angry, To Be Upset

To Be Excluded   *See:* To Discard

Just as snow will cover a sidewalk, so someone who **gives a snow job** is likely to be covering up the truth by exaggerating the facts. To put it still another way, that exaggerator is **full of hot air**.

Eat like a bird

To Fail   miss the boat, fall apart, go over like a lead balloon, go sour like spoiled milk, go down the tube 16, go down the drain, go kerfooey (pronounced *kerr foo ee*), blow it, spin one's wheels.

To fail miserably: miss by a mile.

To admit failure: throw in the towel 16.

   See also: To Disappear, To Be Upset

To Be Familiar   familiar as the back of your hand, familiar as your own face, familiar as your own front door.

To Be Fast   *See:* To Be Quick, To Hurry Up

To Be Fat   fat as a stuffed turkey, fat as a pig, fat as an owl, fat as a big bubble.

Both **down the tubes** and **throw in the towel** mean to fail. Both are sports terms. The first describes a surfer's failure to catch a ride on an ocean wave. The second comes from the custom of throwing a boxer's towel into the ring when he's lost.

16

To Be Favored   be the apple of someone's eye, get the red carpet treatment , get the VIP treatment (pronounced *vee eye pea,* for very important person) 17, be someone's main pal, on someone's short list 17.

To Be Fearful   *See:* To Be Scared

To Be Fed Up   *See:* To Be Disgusted

To Be Ferocious   ferocious as a hungry lion, fierce as a bull, fierce as a fever.

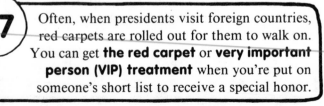

17 Often, when presidents visit foreign countries, red carpets are rolled out for them to walk on. You can get **the red carpet** or **very important person (VIP) treatment** when you're put on someone's short list to receive a special honor.

Free as a bird let out of a cage

To Fight   *See:* To Disagree

To Fit   fit like the skin of a banana, belong like a fish in water, fit like a key in a lock, fit like a hand in a glove.
   See also: To Go Together

To Be Flat   flat as a pancake, flat as a pressed flower, flat as a board.

To Flatter   sweet talk, butter up.
   To flatter without really meaning it: pay a back-handed compliment, soft soap.

To Follow   follow like Monday after Sunday, follow like a shadow, follow someone around like a fly.

To Be Forgetful   *See:* Memory

To Be Free   footloose and fancy free **18**, free as the wind, free as hot air in July, free as a bird let out of a cage.

Footloose and fancy free both begin with the same sound and both mean *freedom.* *Footloose* refers to freedom from rules and regulations and *fancy free* to freedom from another person's influence.

To be free from blame: off the hook.

To free oneself: cut loose.

To be free to go ahead: the coast is clear, it's a go.

To Be Fresh   fresh as a new coat of paint, fresh as bread right out of the oven, fresh as fruit salad.

> *See also:* To Be Current (to give these phrases a different meaning)

To Be Friendly   friendly as a puppy, pal around with, friendly as a *Welcome* sign, friendly as a *Welcome* mat.

To have a close friendship: thick as thieves, to be very tight.

Boy-and-girl friendliness: going out.

To include someone in your group of friends: put in the loop.

Gentle   *See:* To Be Kind

To Be Gloomy   *See:* To Be Sad, To Spoil

To Be Good-Looking   *See:* To Be Nice Looking

To Go On   last like a nightmare, endless as the line around a circle.

To Go Together   go together like hugs and kisses, go together like paper and pencil, get on like peanut butter and jelly.

   See also: To Fit

Green   green as a salad, green as grass, green as spinach, green with envy.

To Be Grouchy   *See:* To Be Sad, To Be Temperamental

To Grow   *See:* To Spread

Get on like peanut butter and jelly

Couldn't fight his way out of a paper bag

To Be Happy   happy as a dog with a bone, happy as a lark.

> **To be extremely happy:**   have the world on a string [19], tickled pink [19], be on Cloud Nine [19], floating on air, out of control.

To Be Hard   tough as nails, tough as an elephant's hide, a tough cookie, hard as a hardboiled egg, hard as frozen gook.

> *See also:* To Be Difficult, Talking

Hard to Catch   *See:* To Avoid

You can't really **have the world on a string** or float **on cloud nine**, but both may seem possible when you're very happy. And neither does someone have to tickle you so that you turn pink from giggling for you to feel **tickled pink** with pleasure.

19

To Be Healthy   sound as a bell [20], fit as a fiddle [20], healthy as a horse [20].

To Help   go to bat for, bail out, pitch in.

To Be Helpless   couldn't fight one's way out of a paper bag, helpless as a bird without wings.
   See also: To Be Weak

To Be Honest   on the up and up, up front, tell it like it is, on the level, to level with someone.

To Be Hostile   *See:* To Be Unfriendly

To Be Hot   hot as a four-alarm fire, hot as a turkey in the oven, hot as X's temper (substitute the name of a temperamental person for "X").

To Be Hungry   hungry as a horse, hungrier than a tapeworm, get the hungries.
   See also: Eating

To Hurry Up   make tracks, shake a leg, get cracking, be somewhere in two shakes, get a move on, step on it, get on the stick, move it, zing along, fast forward.
   See also: To Be Boring

To leave in a hurry: cut out.
   See also: To Be Quick

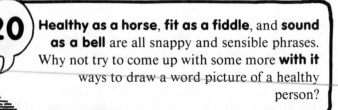

20 Healthy as a horse, fit as a fiddle, and sound as a bell are all snappy and sensible phrases. Why not try to come up with some more **with it** ways to draw a word picture of a healthy person?

To Be Ignorant   ignorant as a snowball, not have a
clue, not have the vaguest.
   See also: To Be Stupid
To Be Important   big deal.
   An important person: a big shot 21, a big deal 21,
      high (or big) muckety-muck, a big cheese.
   Say someone or something is very important   (also
      used as an insult to mean the opposite)**:** big shot
      . . .dot the "i"!
         See also: To Be Favored, Insults, To Be Neces-
         sary, To Be Unimportant
To Be Inactive   *See:* To Be Lazy

Carrying or using a gun has very little to do
with being a **big shot.** And you can turn any **big
shot** or **big deal** into a **big nothing** (*see* Unimportant) if you say the word *big* as if you were
underlining it with red pencil.

21

To Be Inattentive   deaf as a post **22** , let one's mind wander like smoke, tune out **22** , in another world.

To Be Insincere   *See:* To Flatter

To Insult   put down, I need you like I need another belly button.

> **To insult someone who behaves badly:**   with friends like you, I don't need enemies.

---

22 If you repeatedly forget to clean up your room, your mother might exclaim, "You'd think you were **deaf as a post**." Of course, you're not in the least deaf. You simply **tuned out** her reminders to do it, like a TV program you didn't like.

To insult someone who makes stupid remarks: you're out of your tree, where were you when they gave out brains?, you've got brains like mashed potatoes, why don't you send your brains out to be sharpened?, you must have your head screwed on wrong, you must have a screw loose, you're losing it (*it* refers to the brain).

To insult someone who pushes you aside: slime be-fore smart, wise guys before nice guys.

> ***See also:*** To Be Important, Talking, To Be Un-necessary or Unimportant Zapping or Giving Smart Answers

To Be Intelligent   *See:* To Be Smart
To Be Irritable   *See:* To Be Angry

A big cheese

To Jump   jump like a kangaroo, jump like a jack-in-the-box, go up and down like an elevator.

   See also: Moving Around

To Be Jumpy   jumpy as a cat, jumpy as a jumping bean.

   See also: To Worry

Jumpy as a cat

To Be Kind gentle as a lamb, kind as Santa Claus, have a heart as big as a mountain, a big mush.
Someone who seems tough but isn't: someone whose bark is sharper than his bite, a big teddy bear.

His bark is sharper than his bite

Sit there like a plant

To Last *See:* To Go On

To Be Lazy lie around like a blanket, sit there like a plant, goof off, sit on one's hands, veg out (pronounce that "veg" as in "vegetable"), a couch potato, doggin' it (like a lazy dog).

To Lie *See:* To Be Dishonest

To Be Lucky hit it big, catch the gold ring , luck out (also used to mean unlucky).

See also: To Succeed

Some merry-go-round concessions give you a chance to grab hold of a gold-colored brass ring. If you're in luck and **catch the gold ring**, you get a free ride.

To Be Mad   fit to be tied, mad as a wet hen, wild as a fire, see red.

    See also: To Be Angry

To Be Magnificent   *See:* To Be Terrific

To Be Mean   mean as a mugger, mean as murder, mean as ptomaine (pronounced *toe main*) poisoning.

    To treat someone cruelly: make hamburger out of, cut to ribbons, stomp on like a doormat, jump on like a trampoline, push away like a chair.

        See also: To Be Unfair

Memory

    Have a bad memory: a memory like Swiss cheese, a memory like a broken computer.

    Have a good memory: a memory like an elephant, a memory like a guy with a grudge, a memory like a computer.

To Make Mistakes   gum up the works, goof up, be off base, mess up.

To be completely mistaken: all wet, way off (base).

To admit that you've made a mistake: own up to.

To Misunderstand   get one's wires crossed.

Moving Around   turn like an electric fan, jump like a kangaroo, hang a left/right, go back and forth like a windshield wiper, buzz around like a fly, go up and down like an elevator.

See also: To Be Jumpy, To Worry

Stomp on like a doormat

To Nag   *See:* To Scold

To Nap   take forty winks, take a catnap.
   See also: To Sleep

To Be Nasty   *See:* To Be Mean

To Be Nearby   a stone's throw away; just a hop, skip, and a jump away; spitting distance.

To Be Neat   everything is shipshape, spic and span, neat as a pin , neat as a brand-new house.
   See also: To Be Clean

To Be Necessary   necessary as dancing shoes to a ballerina, necessary as fins to a fish, need like a termite needs wood.
   See also: To Be Important

Everyone agrees that to be **neat as a pin** is to be very neat indeed, even though opinions differ about how the phrase became part of our language. Some say it comes from bowling pins; others trace it to sewing pins.

24

Pretty as a picture

To Be Negative   *See:* To Be Sad, To Spoil

To Be Nervous   *See:* To Be Excited, To Be Upset

Never   over my dead body, not on your life, not in a
zillion years.

   See also: To Refuse, To Be Unlikely

To Be New   *See:* To Be Current, To Be Fresh

To Be Nice Looking   pretty as a picture, pretty as a
butterfly, pretty as a parakeet, easy on the eyes, looking
chilly, hot looking.

   See also: To Be Dressed Up

To Be Noisy   so noisy you can't hear yourself think,
noisy as a screaming match, noisy as a thunderstorm.

*As out of place as a baby
on a motorcycle*

To Obey   obedient as a circus lion, toe the mark, knuckle under 25.

To Be Obvious   *See:* To Be Clear

To Be Old-Fashioned   belong in a museum, a golden oldie, not with it.

To Be Ordinary   *See:* To Be Familiar, To Be Simple

To Be Out of Place   feel like a fifth wheel, feel like a fish out of water, belong like a pigeon in a goldfish bowl, belong like a left shoe on a right foot, belong like sugar on spaghetti, out of place as a baby on a motorcycle.

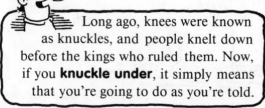

Long ago, knees were known as knuckles, and people knelt down before the kings who ruled them. Now, if you **knuckle under**, it simply means that you're going to do as you're told.

Ready as a pigeon for bread crumbs

To Be Persistent   *See:* To Be Determined
Pink   pink as cotton candy, pink as strawberry ice
   cream, pink as cooked pastrami.
To Please   turn on.
To Be Popular   *See:* To Be Favored

To Praise Something or Someone   you bet, you
said it, way to go, all *right*! (Put everything you've got on
"right"), for shure (pronounced *shurr*).
   See also: To Agree, To Encourage

To Be Prepared   psyched up/out, ready as a pigeon
for bread crumbs.

To Be Proud   *See:* To Be Vain

To Pursue   *See:* To Follow

To Be Puzzling   *See:* To Be Confusing

To Quarrel *See:* To Argue

To Be Quiet so quiet you could hear a pin drop, quiet as a cockroach, quiet as a thought, quiet as dust, quiet as the "p" in pneumonia.

Quiet because one doesn't know what to say: dumb as a stick of wood, dumb as a doorknob, dumb as a dodo bird, dumb as a snowball.

To tell someone to be quiet: zip it, button your lip, button it up, put a cork in it.

    See also: To Be Stupid

Zip it

To Be Quick   quick on the draw, not let grass grow under one's feet, go through like a clown through a hoop, fast as a propeller, fast as a rocket ship, faster than Superman, faster than a speeding bullet, a speed demon.

To do quickly: quick as lightning, quick as going through the X's in the phone book, fast as blinking an eye.

    See also: To Hurry Up

Be in a Rage *See:* To Be Angry

Be Rare rare as a black cow with a white face, rare as a scowling Santa, rare as a black swan, once in a blue moon [26].

Be Ready *See:* To Be Prepared

Be Real real as a toothache, no kidding about it, real as a punch in the nose.

d red as a rose, red as a blush, red as a radish.

Refuse To Do thanks, but no thanks, nothing doing, no way.

See also: Never

Be Regular regular as a clock's tick, regular as a heartbeat, regular as mom's kisses.

According to astrologers, you may indeed see blue moon, but only rarely. It's visible about nce every two years and only in a month during which two full moons occur. No wonder that **nce in a blue moon** events are very nusual. **26**

Rare as a black cow with a white face

To Reject *See:* To Discard

To Relax *See:* To Be Lazy

To Resemble *See:* To Be Alike

To Be Restless *See:* Moving Around

To Ridicule *See:* To Tease

To Be Right right as rain, on the beam, on the right
wave length

    To be exactly right: on the button, to a "T", on the
money.

      See also: To Agree

To Be Ridiculous *See:* To Be Silly

Rare as a black swan

To Ruin *See:* To Spoil
Running *See:* Moving Around
To Rush jump the gun **27** , jump (or go) off the deep
end.

    See also: To Be Quick

If you begin a test before the teacher gives the
go-ahead signal, you're **jumping the gun**, like a
horse that rushes ahead without waiting for
the gun shot that is the official go-ahead signal in
a horse race.

To Be Sad   gloomy as a ghost, act like a dog that's lost its tail, down in the mouth, have a hangdog look, in the dumps, in a funk, down and out.

   To be extremely sad: in a blue funk.

To Be Satisfied   *See:* To Be Happy

To Be Savage   *See:* To Be Ferocious

To Be Scared   have the backbone of a chocolate eclair, have a yellow streak, get cold feet, scared silly, scared out of a year's growth, scared stiff, scared of one's own shadow, scared spitless, scared out of one's wits.

   See also: To Be Upset

Act like a dog that's lost its tail

To Scold   read someone the riot act 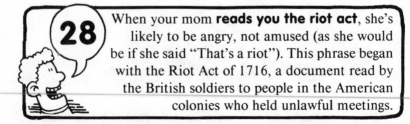 **28**, get a tongue lashing, get on someone's case, get on someone's back, give someone the business.

To be scolded: get chewed out, get one's lumps.

Secretly   on the *q.t.*

To keep something secret: keep under one's hat, keep under wraps, have a mouth like a double lock.

To Be Sensible   *See:* To Be Smart

To Be Serious   *See:* To Be Determined

To Be Shocked   *See:* To Be Surprised

To Show Off   ham it up.

To Be Sick   under the weather.

    See also: To Be Weak

To Be Silent   *See:* Talking

    See also: To Be Useless

To Be Silly   silly as putting water in a basket, silly as math without numbers, silly as a mouse dancing with an elephant, for the birds.

To Be Similar   *See:* To Be Alike

To Be Simple   plain vanilla.

To Be Sincere   *See:* To Be Honest

To Sleep   catch some *Zs,* hit the sack **29**.

To fall asleep from exhaustion: crash out, poop out.

28   When your mom **reads you the riot act**, she's likely to be angry, not amused (as she would be if she said "That's a riot"). This phrase began with the Riot Act of 1716, a document read by the British soldiers to people in the American colonies who held unlawful meetings.

*Not have enough
brains to come
in out of the rain*

To sleep soundly: sleep like a log, sack out , sleep tight.

To snore while you sleep: saw wood.

      See also: To Nap

To Be Slippery   *See:* To Avoid, To Be Smooth

Long ago people slept in sacks that had to be tied in place tightly each night. Even though bed sacks are no longer used, we still **hit the sack** or **sack out** and hope to **sleep tight**.

To Be Sloppy Looking   look like something the cat dragged in, look like a bundle of dirty laundry, dress like a dirtbag, wrinkled as lettuce.

See also: To Be Nice Looking

To Be Slow   slow as sludge, slow as catsup, drag one's feet.

To be very slow: slow as sledding uphill.

To tell someone to slow down: hold your horses, easy does it, cool your jets.

To Be Small   no bigger than a flea, small as a breadcrumb, as big as your thumbnail.

To Be Smart   smart as a whip, smart as an encyclopedia, sharp as a tack, a smart cookie **30**, know which way the wind blows **30**, know the ropes **30**, on the ball **30**, use one's head, quick on the uptake, mega brill (short for brilliant).

See also: To Be Attentive, To Be Current

To Be Smooth   slick as wet soap, slick as spit.

To Be Soft   soft as a kiss, soft as a feather, soft as slime, soft as slush.

To Be Soft-hearted   *See:* To Be Kind

Sounds   *See:* To Be Noisy, To Be Quiet

To Spoil   crumb (or crum) up, glum things up.

Someone who's a spoiler: a wet blanket **31**, a worry wart, a party pooper.

See also: To Be Sad

30   A smart friend can be on the **ball** without being a ball player, **know the ropes** without being a cowboy, or **know which way the wind blows** without being a sailor.

To Spread   spread like germs, spread like a rumor.

To Be Still   still as a suit on a hanger, still as a statue.

Stick To   stick like glue, stick like chewing gum to your shoe, cling to like a stain.

To be sticky: sticky as honey.

To Stop   back off, cut it out, cut it, knock it off, butt out, come off it.

>   *See also:* To Discourage, Zapping or Giving Smart Answers

To Be Straight   straight as an arrow, straight as a ruler, straight as a column of numbers, straight as a soldier's back.

Strange   *See:* To Be Rare

To Be Strong   strong as a hammer, strong as a bull, strong as a weight lifter.

To Be Stubborn   *See:* To Be Determined

To Be Stupid   not know beans, a bird brain, soft in the head, a dim bulb, know zilch, have nothing upstairs, not have brains enough to come in out of the rain, a mini-mind.

>   *See also:* To Be Quiet

To Succeed   get on the fast track, pan out, make the grade, make the loop.

To be especially successful: make it with flying colors.

>   *See also:* To Win

It's nice to snuggle under a nice warm blanket, but a wet one would definitely spoil the fun. With this picture in mind, it's not hard to figure out that a **wet blanket** is a spoilsport.

Strong as a weight lifter

Sudden   sudden as a sneeze, sudden as a stitch in your side.

   How a sudden action affects someone: hit like a ton of bricks, knock one's socks off.

   See also: To Be Surprised

To Be Sure Of   *See:* To Be Certain

To Be Surprised   knocked for a loop, surprised (or shocked) to one's toes.
   Something surprising: surprising as snow in July, surprising as salt on a doughnut.
To Be Suspicious   smell a rat.
To Be Sweet   sweet as honey, sweet as your mom saying "yes, you can."

To Be Talented *See:* To Be Smart

Talking

    To talk up: sing out.

    To talk tough: beat it, buzz off, go take a walk, go suck an egg, push off, you're dead, get lost, get out of my face, bite moose.

    To talk too much: talk a blue streak, talk someone's ear off, run off at the mouth, shoot off one's mouth.

    To talk very little: silent as a clam, silent as a snowflake, silent as dust, silent as the "h" in ghost, zip one's lip.

    To talk well: have the gift of gab, be a smooth talker.

    To talk stupidly: put one's foot in one's mouth.

    To talk things over: chew the rag, shoot the breeze.

        See also: Insults, Zapping or Giving Smart Answers

To Be Tall tall as a tower, tall as a skyscraper, tall as a totem pole.

        See also: To Be Big

Thin as a flagpole

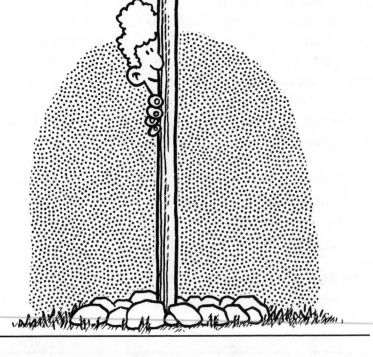

To Be a Tattletale spill the beans, mouth on someone, blab off.

To Tease pull someone's leg.

To tease and be annoying: poke fun at, jerk someone's chain.

To Be Temperamental have a short fuse.

To Be Terrific amazingly awesome, totally rad, the
best ever, out of this world, out of sight.

To Be Thin thin as a stick, thin as spaghetti, thin as a
thread, thin as a pin, thin as a flagpole.

To Be Thorough *See:* Completely

To Throw Away *See:* To Discard

To Be Timely *See:* To Be Current

To Be Tired feel all washed up, feel wiped out, feel all
beat up, pooped out, worn out, zonked out, crumped
out, fuzzed out, knocked out, played out, weak as a
wet rag, weak as a cooked noodle.

    See also: To Be Sick, To Be Weak

To Think work out your brain, noodle around.

To think hard: rack one's brain 32 .

To Be Tough *See:* To Be Hard, Talking

To Be Tricky funny business, tricky as a magician,
tricky as running on ice.

When we talk about **racking our brain** we're
stretching it out only in our imagination. That
wasn't the case hundreds of years ago, when
torture racks were used to make people confess
to wrongdoings.

To Be in Trouble   on the spot **33**, in a tight spot, in a pickle, in a jam, in hot water, put one's foot in it, up a tree, up against the wall, in a bind.

To make trouble: make waves.

See also: To Be In Disgrace

To Try   go out on a limb, give something a go, give something your all, have a go at.

33 To be put **on the spot** has been used since 1723 when the writer Jonathan Swift made up this rhyme:
If once they get you on the spot, you must plead guilty of the plot.

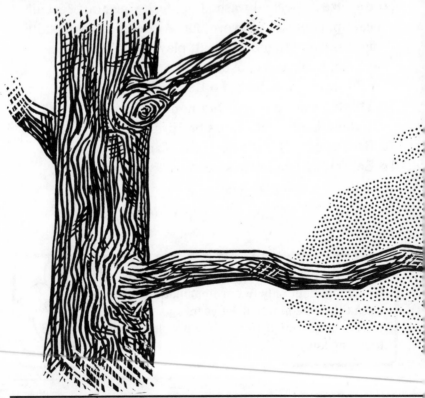

To try extremely hard: go all out , knock oneself out, leave no stone unturned, stand on one's head trying .

To try to do more than possible: bite off more than one can chew.

To try or do something even if it's risky: take the plunge, go out on a limb.

To urge someone to try: do it, go for it.

To urge someone to keep trying: hang in there.

> *See also:* To Encourage

Turning   *See:* Moving Around

> We all know some kid who may not be the best ball player, but who would **go all out** trying—the kind of kid who would **stand on his head trying**, if he thought that would work.

34

Out on a limb

To Be Uncomfortable   uncomfortable as a stone mattress, uncomfortable as a bicycle without a seat.

To Be Undecided   on the fence, up in the air.

To Understand   get the hang of something, get it.

   To understand a person: know what makes someone tick, read someone like a book, read someone loud and clear.

      See also: To Be Clear

To Be Unenthusiastic   couldn't care less (or, could care less), not give a rap, not give squat, not give spit, not give a hoot.

      See also: To Be Unnecessary or Unwanted

To Be Unexciting   *See:* To Be Boring

To Be Unfair   do someone dirty, deal a low blow, hit below the belt, down and dirty, take a cheap shot, do a number on someone, stab in the back.

To Be Unfriendly   give a cold shoulder, give the brush-off, give the air, act like a cold fish, to freeze out,

*Bent out
of shape*

to frost someone, not give the time of day, put the chill on, have an attitude.

    See also: To Be Cold

To Be Unimportant   no big deal, a big nothing, not count for spit.

    Something that was important but no longer is: *X'ed* out.

    See also: Zapping or Giving Smart Answers

To Be Uninteresting *See:* To Be Boring

To Be Unlikely   that will be the day, as likely as a snow storm in July, fat chance.

    See also: Never

To Be Unnecessary or Unwanted   need like a hole in the head, need like a third nostril, welcome as a belly-ache, as much fun as a fever.

    See also: To Insult, To Be Useless

Untruthful *See:* To Be Dishonest

To Be Upset   bent out of shape, come unstuck, hit the panic button, get into a sweat.

    To cause something to be upset: upset the apple cart, throw for a loop.

    See also: To Be Angry

To Be Up-to-date *See:* To Be Current

To Be Useful useful as a pocket in a shirt.

To Be Useless useful as a bike without tires, useless as a single glove, useless as a chocolate teapot.

To Be Vain   vain as a peacock, act like God's gift, full of one's self.

To Vanish vanish into thin air, vanish like writing in the sand.

   See also: To Disappear

To Be Violent   *See:* To Be Ferocious

Vanish into thin air

A bookhound

To Waste Time   twiddle your thumbs, hack around, futz around.

To Be Weak   *See:* To Be Tired

White   white as snow, white as a ghost, white as an uncooked chicken, white as a cloud.

   See also: To Be Boring

To Win

  To win in a big way: beat the socks off someone, win by a mile.

  To just about win: beat by a hair.

    See also: To Succeed

To Be Wonderful   *See:* To Be Terrific

To Work Hard   use lots of elbow grease, knuckle down, crack the books, wonk out, nerd out, plug along, work up a sweat, a bookhound.

   See also: To Try

To Worry   jumpy as a cat, sweat bullets, in a sweat, worry like a mouse in a trap.

   See also: To Be Scared

Scream like cats in a dark alley

Yelling and Screaming scream like cats in a dark alley, scream like a fire engine, scream like a hurricane.

    See also: To Be Noisy

Yellow yellow as a lemon, yellow as corn on the cob.

    See also: To Be Scared

Zapping or giving smart answers

Zapping or Giving Smart Answers

Zapping liars and boasters: you're all wet, you lie like a stone, that's a crock, take your big brain and shove it.

Zapping someone who talks too much or too tough: watch it.

Zapping someone you disagree with: you're out of your bird, give me a break, you've got to be kidding (put extra strength into *got*), get real.

Zapping someone who insults or teases: very funny (put everything you've got on *very*), you forgot to make me laugh, that's *sooo* funny, sticks and stones 35.

See also: Insults, Talking, To Be Dishonest, To Be Unimportant

Sticks and stones is a shorter version of this little rhyme: Sticks and stones may break my bones, but words will never harm me.

From Phrase Seeker to Phrase Maker

People are constantly searching for ways to change and improve the way we live. And as things change, so does our language. That's why we hope that you'll keep this book of phrases up-to-date by writing down and using interesting new phrases that you hear *and* that you make up yourself.

Getting Started as a Phrase Maker

One of the easiest ways to develop your ability to make up original phrases is to use the phrases in this thesaurus as a starting point. Here's how it works.

Suppose you want to tell someone something is boring. Easy. Turn to **To Be Boring**, under the letter "B". You could borrow *boring as boiled potatoes,* but why not see if you can think of something besides boiled potatoes that would make you yawn. Got it? Congratulations, you've just created a phrase of your own and are eligible to join FACTS, the Fresh And Colorful Talk Society.

You can also change phrases under one heading to fit another meaning. To see how this is done let's go back to our search for a phrase to describe a boring person or activity. This time go to the heading **To Be Important**, under the letter "I". What's the idea of being important got to do with being boring? Well, if you borrow from *big shot . . . dot the "i"* used to compliment or insult, you've got this possibility: *boring . . . make that boring with a capital "B"*!

As you can see it's really as easy as...as easy as what? Go on, think of something really easy (and don't peek under **To Be Easy).**

Some Phrase-Making Tips

Now that you've learned how easy it is to give an existing phrase an original twist, here are a few dos and don'ts to keep in mind both when you "reinvent" an existing phrase or invent one from scratch:

1. Don't use a phrase, no matter how much you like it, unless it's the right phrase for the right occasion. It's okay to tell a friend to *get real* or to *chill out,* but such slang expressions might not please your teacher.
2. To add snap, crackle, and pop to an expression, try beginning it with words that say the opposite of what you mean. For example, instead of *useless as two left shoes* you could say *useful as two left shoes.* The complimentary phrase used as an insult (like *big shot* or *big deal*) is another example of this method.
3. To call extra attention to an idea, try using two similar expressions instead of just one. To make it clear that something is finished or has disappeared, you could say *it's gone like smoke.* To give your expression an extra bang, you could follow it with a different phrase that says the same thing, for example: *It's gone like smoke. . . like raindrops in a drain.* In the same way, to convince

someone that your friend Billy is very good-natured, you might say that he's *a real marshmallow, a big mush.* Two important points to keep in mind when you use this technique for adding emphasis are (a) don't overdo it and (b) do be sure that each phrase you use describes the same thing.

4. Remember that the most colorful expressions actually draw a picture of what they mean. Therefore, always check your expressions to see if your word picture makes sense. One of our junior editors turned the familiar *busy as a bee* into *busy as a frisbee.* Nice as this sounded, it didn't make sense to the other editors. You see, a bee buzzes about busily all on its own, but a frisbee is an object that doesn't move unless you pick it up and toss it. After thinking it over, our phrase-maker came up with *busy as a frisbee at the beach*! This time everybody got the picture!

Someone else came up with *busy as a bouncing ball* which adds sound appeal through alliteration. (Remember, alliterative phrases have two or more words that begin with the same sound.) Maybe now is a good time to go back and read the Introduction. While you're at it, take another look at the very beginning of the book, which contains an invitation to become a Kids' World Almanac Junior Editor.

Index

This index includes every *phrase* in the phrase section in letter-by-letter alphabetical order. In alphabetizing the phrases, the following words were omitted: *a, an, the, to* and *to be*. Some phrases are entered by more than one key word; for example, **all dolled up** is also entered as **dolled up**.

A

I